Reference plans ▶
showing photograph
vantage points
inside

Additional plans
◀◀ inside front cover

Ledge House

Bohlin Cywinski Jackson

Edited by Oscar Riera Ojeda
Introduction by William P. Bruder
Photographs by Karl A. Backus

Rockport Publishers
Gloucester, Massachusetts

SINGLE BUILDING Series | Process of an Architectural Work

First published in the
United States of America by:
Rockport Publishers, Inc.
33 Commercial Street
Gloucester, Massachusetts 01930-5089
Telephone: (978) 282-9590
Facsimile: (978) 283-2742

Distributed to the book trade
and art trade in the United States by:
North Light Books, an imprint of
F & W Publications
1507 Dana Avenue
Cincinnati, Ohio 45207
Telephone: (800) 289-0963

Other Distribution by:
Rockport Publishers, Inc.
Gloucester, Massachusetts 01930-5089

ISBN 1-56496-521-X

10 9 8 7 6 5 4 3 2 1

Printed in China

Numbers in bold for each photograph correspond to

vantage point numbers on site and floor plans found

on the inside front and back cover flaps.

Cover & Front Matter Captions

Cover:	**1** Entry at dusk
Page 2/3:	**2** Forecourt and north wall from the northwest
Page 4/5:	**3** Living space from entry
Page 7:	**4** West end at dusk
Page 9:	**5** View of master bedroom during construction

contents

Ledge House

by William Bruder

Pragmatism produces shelter, while the pursuit of poetry results in the creation of art. For architecture to exist, poetry and pragmatism must approach perfect balance. Such is the case in this charismatic weekend house in the mountains of Maryland by Peter Bohlin and his associates at Bohlin Cywinski Jackson. ▮ My introduction to the house came when I was exploring the romance and tectonics of log construction for a project of my own. I had talked to local craftsmen and looked to architectural history, seeking the masterful use of logs and finding Robert Redmer's Old Faithful Inn of 1903 in Yellowstone Park, and Reima Pietila's Saresto Gallery of 1972, near the Arctic Circle in Lapland. Then I saw sketches and construction photos of this house. Immediately drawn to it, I made two trips to see it in person, and my greatest expectations were surpassed. It is therefore with great pleasure that I share my thoughts about this inventive and masterful creation. ▮ Real architecture is a challenging celebration of the client, the context, the greater community, the craft of construction and its metaphysical as well as physical presence. Without clients, architecture cannot exist. When a client and an architect challenge each other with ideas in the pursuit of excellence, magic results. ▮ In the case of this weekend retreat, a family's physical needs have resulted in a house with the quality of a thoughtful but ordinary country cabin or cottage, yet also a rigorously sophisticated investigation of architectural imagination. The owner's dedication to life, ideas, and quality is evident everywhere, brought to life by the skill of the architects. At every turn, the architects have answered more than the client's program. ▮ The building is grounded firmly in its natural setting. Neighboring structures—humble homes, barns and sheds—speak of hundreds of years

of habitation in simple combinations of stone and wood; their common-sense plans, massing, and joinery possess mysterious

power and elegance. Viewed through the trees, Bohlin Cywinski Jackson's house also conveys a sense of having always been

there. In the entry forecourt this sense of fit is even more powerful. The stone foundations anchoring the scheme to the land

have both archaeological and geological power. The gathering and assemblage of the massive stones call to mind ruins, or

primitive, not contemporary, construction. Abstract and massive, the stonework powerfully marries building and site. With

similar primal vigor the logs at the arrival court seem to grow naturally from the site, forming the edge of what feels like

a prehistoric ceremonial platform, or a sunlit quarry. ▌ The house embodies the quiet and privacy desired by the owner yet

stands proudly in the context of the great residences of the twentieth century. While completely original, the design has roots

in the work of Frank Lloyd Wright, Mies van der Rohe, Alvar Aalto and Louis I. Kahn; it also captures the mastery and

eccentric unpredictability of the Swedish architect Sigurd Lewerentz. In the way Lewerentz's Church of St. Peter at Klippen,

Sweden uses the simplicity of uncut brick, Bohlin's retreat uses stone and log with tectonic and spiritual resolve. ▌ Craft is

implicit in every joint, detail, and finish. That the carpenters, stone masons and other technicians were all local further bonds

the project to its place. The traditions and skills of nearby buildings empower the concepts and invention here. Process, logic,

appropriateness, and weathering all strengthen decisions about materials and assembly. Each juncture is lovingly conceived and

patiently assembled. Each photo, each drawn detail shows a delight in the meeting of log and stone, column and beam, saddle and bolt, cladding and glazing, toward an ideal meeting of land and sky. ▌ Finally, in the choreography of the parts

and the whole lies a pragmatic and poetic power that is mysterious and memorable. The logic and order of plan and section

are set in tension against playful and unexpected juxtapositions of scale, proportion, structure, transparency and movement.

The experience of the house is thus enriched by the thoughtful and the unexpected, the raw and the beautiful. The house is

so carefully thought out and assembled that it is carefree in use and habitation. It is architecture of its time that aspires to

timelessness. ▌ In this work, extremes, edges, and eccentricity combine to form an original, inspired whole. This is a moment

at a clearing in the woods where stone meets log, idea meets reality, invention meets craft, function meets beauty, and

the past meets the present. It is a place where the magic of architecture inspires one to relax and dream what might be!

William Bruder ▌ New River, Arizona ▌ December 22, 1997

William Bruder is an artist/architect who has worked for the past twenty-five years from a desert studio in New River, Arizona. His architecture is a search for pragmatic and poetic solutions to site opportunities and user needs, craftsman-like in its concern for detail and process, sculptural in its blending of materials, space, and light. He believes architecture is the celebration of listening in the service of the human spirit and senses.

We believe in an architecture that reveals the particular nature of its circumstance: the nature of its place, both natural and man-made, ranging from the nature and history of a region to the particular qualities of a site—the topography, tilt, warp, flatness of the land; the scale, texture, denseness, and openness of its landscape—the sun and its arc over the place and the corresponding bright and muted light, the breezes and sounds of the place, the memories of other places far and nearby; the nature of people, all of us, especially those who will be in the place—how we move, touch, feel, and see, how we participate in the place, what we do there, what we remember of other places, and how we react to the natural and to the man-made; and, of course, the nature of how we make things—the materials we use, how they come together, how they speak of their origins, their will to organize spaces, and their interplay. ▮ With both reason and intuition, we seek to discover the connections among all these things; the connection between the quite tangible aspects of a place and the more elusive feelings it prompts; how we approach and inhabit it; how a building might resonate in its place. ▮ We are interested in the connection between a material and the place it quite naturally makes. All things have a kind of will. Stone sits; we feel its weight. It is of the earth; we often see how it was formed. Wood can be both skin and structure. It is most often linear in nature, making orthogonal spaces that have a grain, spaces that have quite different faces and sides. Wood floats, makes rafts. Wood shrinks, binds, and warps. The making of its connections is fascinating. What do materials say of their past, their will? Beginnings and endings interest us, whether of a journey, or a column with its top and bottom, or the end of a handrail. ▮ We believe in an

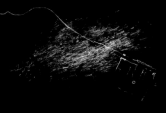

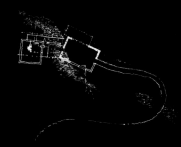

Bohlin Summer House, West Cornwall, Connecticut, photograph and preliminary sketch (above) Bill Gates residential compound, Medina, Washington (top right) House in the Endless Mountains, Lake Winola, Pennsylvania, photograph and preliminary sketch (bottom right)

architecture that tells us the nature of its place, its use, its making; that can be read intellectually yet speaks to our unconscious; that is both clear and elusive; that offers insights; that enables and liberates us. These interests are threaded throughout our lives and our practice. ▌ For me, many of these thoughts are rooted in my years at Rensselaer and Cranbrook. There, my drive to get at the truths that underlie the web of circumstance surrounding the making of places crystallized. Over the past 30 years, many people within our practice have extended these interests, which continue to inform our architecture.

▌ **Antecedents** Bohlin Cywinski Jackson has enjoyed doing a wide variety of projects, ranging from modest houses and camps to large private and public commissions. And, although our practice has become national in scope, I personally continue to delight in making houses. I enjoy their unusually complex and individual circumstances and the opportunity to reveal the subtle nature of a place. I work on each house with younger architects from our practice and feel we have learned lessons together that affect our larger projects. These architects go on to manage major assignments that incorporate issues first glimpsed in the houses. ▌ The summer house Russ Roberts and I did for my parents in 1974 is approached through a dark evergreen forest and extends into a sunlit, deciduous woodland. It is all about getting from here to there. It is a touching house made with modest materials. ▌ In 1991, Robert McLaughlin and I designed a house in Pennsylvania's Endless Mountains that is approached through a series of stone foundations and courts. The house explored the use of milled heavy timber and its connections. ▌ At the same time, we were working with James Cutler Architects on the residential compound for Bill Gates

Pool Pavilion, Montgomery County, Pennsylvania; photograph and preliminary sketch (above) House in the Adirondacks, upstate New York; column detail, sketch, entry view and interior view (opposite page)

in the Pacific Northwest. Theresa Thomas and Bill Loose, both senior architects from our practice, joined Jim and me and people from both offices on what was a very special design opportunity. The Gates guest house slides through the landscape, again moving from here to there, revealing the shift in landscape and outlook. Working with superb, milled, recycled timber, we refined our thoughts about the timber's steel feet and connections. ∎ In 1992, Don Maxwell and I worked on a pool in Pennsylvania that bordered a stone wall and extended into the landscape. It is dream-like, blurring the edge between the man-made and the natural. ∎ Perhaps the project most closely related to the house in the Maryland mountains was done in 1988, when Royce Earnest, Robert McLaughlin, and I designed a house in the Adirondacks that was more literally in the nature of the Great Camps, yet slyly inventive. Its crafted nature and gabled roofs are very much in the spirit of the Great Camps, which were inspired by European alpine buildings and Japanese architecture. Rooted in the landscape with a base and fireplace made of great stone boulders, the house has white cedar columns and beams from nearby trees. It also uses a sliding, Modernist geometry in plan and separates skin and structure. Harvey Kaiser, author of *The Great Camps of the Adirondacks*, had suggested that we be the architects for this house.   ∎ **Beginnings** The site of the house in the mountains of Maryland is a remarkable landscape of forests, mountainsides, stone ledges, and clear trout streams. Our clients were particularly fond of the evocative qualities found in many Adirondack buildings of the early part of this century—an architecture of stone, logs and heavy timber. They asked Harvey Kaiser for his advice, and he suggested several architects, again including us. ∎ We

walked the mountain in Maryland and chose a manmade ledge cut into the hillside that had been the site of a cabin built in the 1940's. The ledge is backed to the north by a dark grove of pine and overlooks a sunlit, deciduous forest that slopes south down to a clear, boulder-strewn trout stream. The sound of the stream as it rushes in spring or after a rain permeates the hillside. The site is approached from the northeast along an existing trail that had been cut along the lower shoulder of the mountain. ▌ Our clients, a couple with two young children, wished to have a house they could retreat to on weekends and holidays that would contrast with their house in suburban Washington. They wished to make a place that would accommodate occasional large gatherings, but would be comfortable for their family of four. They asked for a living/dining/kitchen space, two children's bedrooms, and a larger master bedroom with related bath and dressing spaces. They asked for a study that, with fold-out bed, could double as a guest room. They wished to have a screened porch adjacent to the living/dining/kitchen area that faced the sun, and since the weather is often chilly in the mountains, they hoped to have an indoor swimming pool. They wished to have fireplaces that served these spaces, and asked if we might make an outdoor place for larger gatherings, picnics and barbecues. ▌ As with our other houses, I worked with architects in our office who focused on this project exclusively. Joe Biondo served as the project manager, and ours was a particularly satisfying relationship. Alan Purvis joined the team later. Our clients were enthusiastic, thoughtful, and encouraging. We all set out to make a calm, yet powerful place in this evocative landscape. ▌ **Insights** We felt that while this house in the Maryland mountains might be made of logs, stone, and heavy,

milled wood timbers, it should not refer too literally to the Great Camps of the Adirondacks. Rather, we believed we might make a stirring place that fit our clients' wishes and revealed the particular nature of its time, place and making. We thought of nearby utilitarian shed structures. ▮ We saw that the experience of approaching the house from the north and then discovering the sunlit forest and stream felt inevitable. We saw that the stone cut in the mountainside was a fine forespace. A place to catch cars and gather people, it could feel like the remains of a quarry one might come upon in the forest. There were hints of this in the stone ledges that were visible at its edge. We felt the house could ring the curved southern rim of this flat place and float off the hillside toward sun, view, and the sound of the stream. We saw that the entire place could become extraordinarily touching. ▮ We saw that we might make a wall between the forespace and the house, a wall that would help define the place—a veil through which one would enter, discovering the forested stream valley below. We considered passing through a wall of stone, then decided to make a veil of stacked horizontal logs. The logs' alternating direction tells us of their origin as tapered trees. They are stabilized by short log crosswalls, so the wall tells us of its making. After considering many species, we chose white cedar for its soft color, stability, and durability. ▮ We saw that this wall could seem to sit on the stone ledge, and that the ledge could slip under the wall into the house, extending the landscape into the living spaces. The ledge's stepped, ragged edge could, quite naturally, provide the opportunity for lounging. The building adapts to the edge. The layers of wood floors float over the stone or are scribed to its edge. The wood floors are never in the same plane as

the stone. We celebrate the essence of these materials. Stone is massive; it extends down into the earth. Wood is light; it floats. It can be scribed to the stone. It can seem like the surface of a body of water against a rocky shore. When wood floats over the stone, we glimpse framing underneath. ▌ We first considered using local stone, but chose a stone from New York's Lake Champlain, since the Champlain material has a similar appearance and is structurally superior and available in much larger pieces. This stone, with its rippled surface, tells us of its origin beneath a shallow inland sea. ▌ The house is a series of spaces that twists around the edge of the stone clearing, following the shape of the land. Backed by log walls, these living spaces open out to the hillside through sunlit forest. They are roofed by tilted rafts of milled timber. The rafts seem to float; they are supported by milled columns for the interior and by natural log columns and beams for the exterior. ▌ Where log walls and beams extend out from under the hovering roofs, they are protected from the weather by lead shrouds that are pounded to their shapes. Like our house in the Adirondacks, the shrouds are somewhat biomorphic. Fabricated metal tongues protect the exposed ends of all milled wood beams. Held free of the beam ends to permit the wood to breathe, these tongues make a rich pattern. ▌ Wood shrinks across its grain. The roof's milled rafts do not touch the horizontal log walls; rather, they cantilever to the north over them. As one approaches the house, the toothed edges of these floating, cantilevered roofs hint at the nature of its interior spaces. The structural grain of the roof plane extends out to the sun and view. ▌ We thought the roof's wood members might tell us of themselves. They slide by each other when their lengths are shorter than the extent of

the roof. The supporting members are doubled when they pick up additional stresses at the angled bracing columns. The rich pattern of the framing is an expression of the stresses within the roof and its materials. To accommodate the angled relationships of the roofs, rafts of the timber are slipped under and over each other. One sees between them. ▮ Beginnings and endings are particularly potent positions. The milled wood columns have metal fittings that seemingly sit on the stone ledge; they have feet. Where columns are angled, the steel feet are wedge shaped. We were also thinking of this base condition at the Gates Residence, but here where these columns land on a wood floor, they slip through the wood plane to the structure below. They slide down into a shadowed reveal. ▮ Steel fittings also connect the columns to the roof's north/south beams. Large springs pull the fittings down as the beams shrink. We considered using this solution at the Gates Residence, but felt it was too demonstrative. It was just right here. While we used a special black patina on the stainless steel fittings at Gates, and we painted the steel fittings dark gray for our house in Pennsylvania's Endless Mountains, we galvanized all the steel for this house. Galvanizing's mottled, slightly crazed finish has more character and tells more of itself. ▮ We designed the window walls to be light and transparent. The mullions are milled wood. To strengthen the taller, thinner members, we stiffened them with light, exposed, galvanized steel splints. The operating casements have a thin metal profile with a finish that is similar to the stiffeners. The shifting, staccato pattern of wood mullions, large sheets of glass, silvery metal operating sash, and intermittent vertical metal stiffeners is delicate and satisfying. ▮ We saw that one could also look up to the north

and the large pine forest. One could sense the shift of sun and the changing quality of light from morning to night through all seasons. We could make a place that would fit the land, a place that would reveal the subtleties of view, light, and sound. ▌ **The Indoors** The entry portal through the log wall is sheltered and marked by an extended roof supported by a log beam and two massive columns. The heavy, wood-plank door is set in planes of glass and slender mullions. My son Nat, with Joe and me, designed a cut-out, rusted-steel armature that projects over the entry like the bough of an evergreen—a floating frieze. ▌ One enters through the shaded north wall. Drawn by the light and view, one moves across the stone ledge and down onto a wood floor into the living/dining space, which is at the heart of the house. The stone ledge twists around to the west, providing seating and the hearth for a massive fireplace built of the same stone as the ledge. With fireplaces in both the living space and an adjacent study and a hollow for wood storage, this primal stone mass was thought of as an outcropping. An angular skylight framed in a spider web of galvanized steel brings light down its stone face. We intended to make this central living/dining space both weighty yet light, sheltered yet open, powerful yet delicate, defined yet elusive. ▌ With Ken Heitz, an Adirondack craftsman, we designed the round wood dining table of plank and natural timber legs and the branch and twig chairs of ironwood. For upholstered seating in the living area, we used the 1920's modernism of Jean Michel Frank. For a desk and a low table, we designed glass tops with fir members of the same dimension as our millwork. We also found American hickory antiques dating back to the early part of this century. ▌ The kitchen, under a skewed, slightly lower roof

plane, is part of this space. A screened porch extends to the south. We saw that the porch could have the essence of a sheltered tree house floating into the forest. From there one looks sideways along the lit faces of the house, as well as out and down through deciduous trees to the stream. ▮ Our clients' bedroom, bath, and study are located beyond the fireplace mass, west of the living space and closest to the stream, with views to the south and through the trees along the mountain slope to the west. The sound of rushing water and the gentle rustle of the forest in the night recall memories of my childhood in northwestern Connecticut. We thought it would be a fine place to lie in bed, looking out to the softly lit evening forest and north up to the dark pines in the evening light. ▮ We remembered the nature of simple cottages with their exposed framing and stud walls skinned on only one side; a revealing way to build. We adapted this approach, using carefully milled, three-inch-thick fir studs. Our clients suggested plywood for interior surfaces. In the master bedroom a pocket door is visible as it slides behind studs into the wall. Its rolling hardware is celebrated. Electrical conduit to industrial switches and receptacles is exposed. ▮ We carefully structured storage cupboards, shelving, and bathroom vanities with light fir framing and fir plywood. They are a kind of crafted De Stijl. Door and cabinet pulls are like metal tongues—somewhat biomorphic. Jim and I first did these at Gates. We gave the vanities metal toes. The wood drawers reveal their dovetailed construction: a metal fitting cradles the towel bar; the slate top sits and floats; the lavatory bowls are round stainless steel dishes—a satisfying exercise. ▮ We designed our clients' bed as part of the house. It nestles into a recessed cabinet/box that floats in a glass wall and projects

out beyond the west face of the bedroom. The box firmly positions the bed in its space. The bed has a seating ledge at its foot. From the hillside forest the view of the master bedroom's west face clearly reveals the nature of the house; the edge of the stone ledges and the hill falling away to the south; the north wall of horizontal logs; the floating tilted plane of its roof supported by milled timbers and log beams and columns at its south face, and the framing of the horizontal floor plane beneath the bed's projected box. ▮ Lying in bed, one can look down a passage of finely framed plywood doors to the study's fireplace. We placed a Gunnar Asplund chair there. We found his framed sketch for that chair and placed it on a shelf in the study. We designed an asymmetrical, fold-out sofa bed that permits one to lounge sideways, looking out to the forest. The study's pocket door slides into a plywood-and-fir cupboard between study and hall. As it slides, it moves across a cupboard window. We designed fireplace tools of steel and leather for the study and living space. ▮ A passage extends east from the house's heart along the face of the log wall. Lit by high north light, it borders the children's bedrooms and baths, arriving at a sliding, galvanized-steel door that opens to the pool. Pocketing into a wood-framed partition, the door has no jamb. Its edge is cut out to fit the profile of the logs and stone ledge. As the door approaches, wall and door speak of each other. We called it the "mouse bite" door. ▮ The pool extends along the stone ledge. As with much of the house, we thought of it as being both inside and outside, defined and elusive. We wished to give one the feeling of swimming in a magical landscape, a dreamlike place. One swims along the stone ledge, looking out to the sunlit forest canopy. Angled columns brace

the roof structure and mark the swimmer's progress. The swimmer can look back through the "mouse bite" door toward the house's heart, while the rhythm of bracing columns extends to the distant entry. ▌ **The Bridge** When the house was nearing completion, our clients asked that we design a foot bridge across the stream. We saw that it must clear spring floods and touch a higher bank on the far side. We felt it should seem light and speak of its nature. We intended it to be both tough-minded and graceful. Joe and I designed an inverted "V" trussed structure in rusted Cor-ten steel. We carefully considered its connections as it springs from bank to bank. The bridge's wood plank surface extends beyond the structure, and its delicate wood and galvanized steel railing echoes the detailing of an inclined rail at the house's entry. As with the house, the bridge's rusted steel, weathered wood and galvanized steel resonate with the colors of the forest stream. ▌ **In Gratitude** We could not have done all of this without Greg Currey, a fine, enthusiastic young contractor, and his men, and, of course, the encouragement of our extraordinary clients. ▌ We all set out to make a house/place that fit its circumstance like a glove; that revealed the particular nature of its place, its inhabitants, and its making: a journey that was both intellectual and intuitive. We grew with this house. We continue to search for these qualities.

Peter Bohlin ▌ Wilkes-Barre, Pennsylvania ▌ December 15, 1997

Peter Bohlin, a founding principal of Bohlin Cywinski Jackson, received a bachelor of architecture degree from Rensselaer Polytechnic Institute and his master's from Cranbrook Academy of Art. A member of the American Institute of Architects, Mr. Bohlin served as chair of the institute's national Committee on Design from 1984 to 1985, and was named a fellow of the AIA in 1981. ▮ Working over the years with a number of young architects in the practice, Peter Bohlin has designed many houses—from a summer house for his parents in 1974, to recent projects such as the William Gates III residential compound (in a joint venture with James Cutler), houses in the Adirondacks, the Endless Mountains of Pennsylvania, and the subject of this book, Ledge House in the mountains of Maryland. ▮ A 1994 AIA Press publication, *The Architecture of Bohlin Cywinski Jackson*, provides a general introduction to the firm's work.

Ledge House

Drawings and Photographs

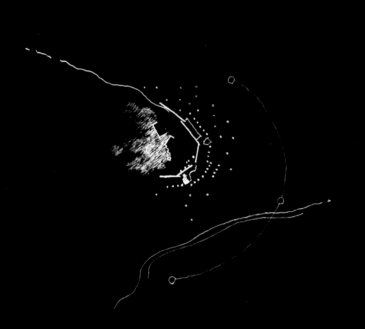

21 Detail: north facade and early study floor plan (previous spread) Conceptual plan and section sketches: site and building (this spread) Early study plan (foldout page)

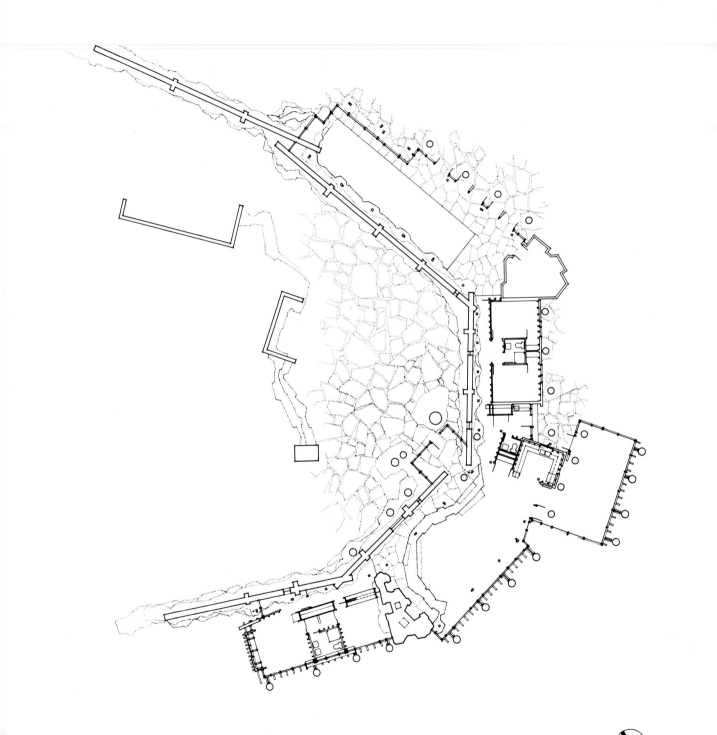

Floor plan

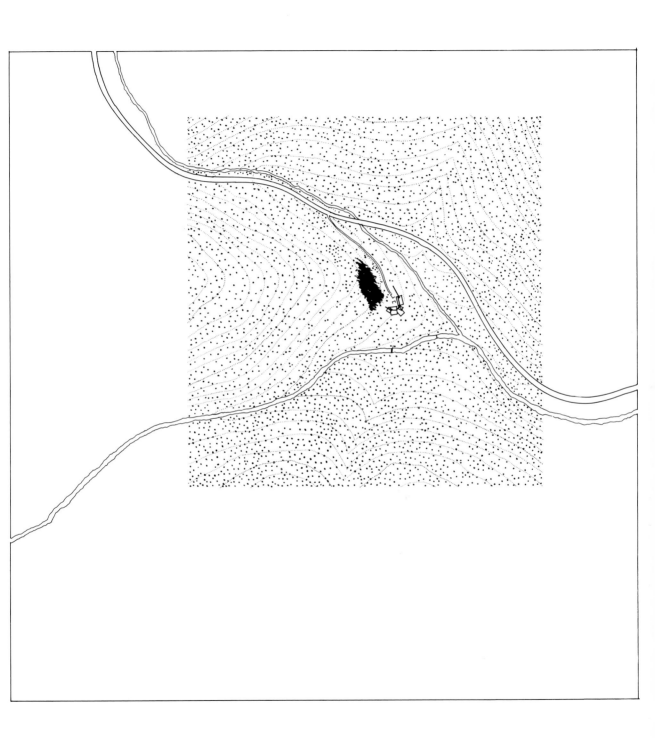

Site plan

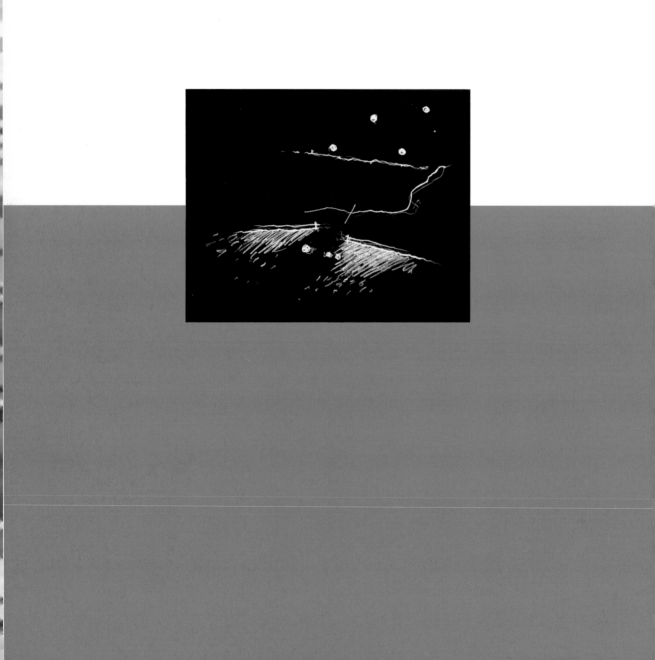

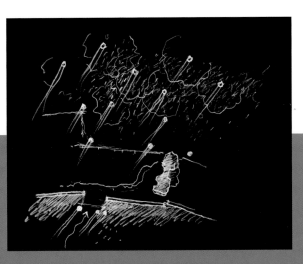

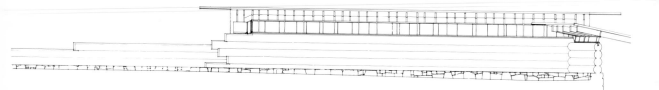

Pool elevation

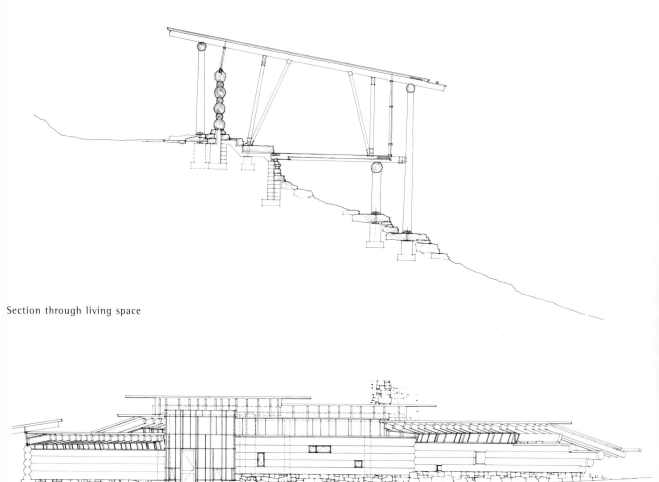

Section through living space

Northwest elevation

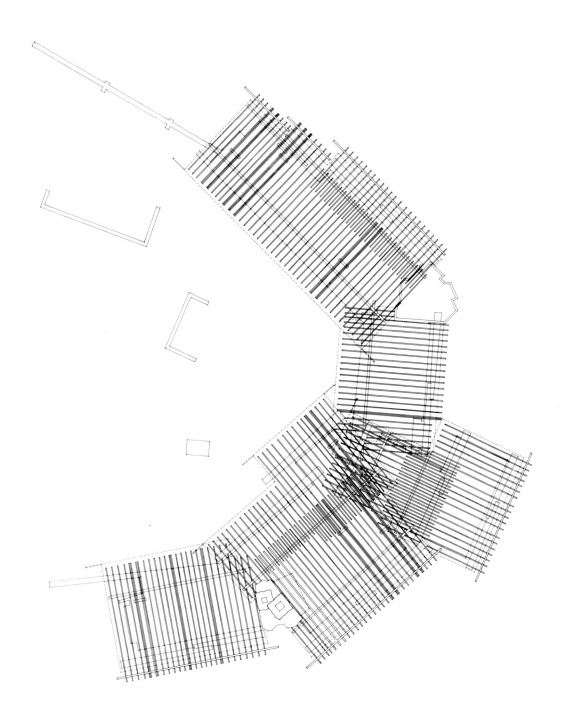

Roof framing plan

Conceptual sketch: plan study (upper right) Sketch: north elevation (lower right) Early plan study (previous foldout page)

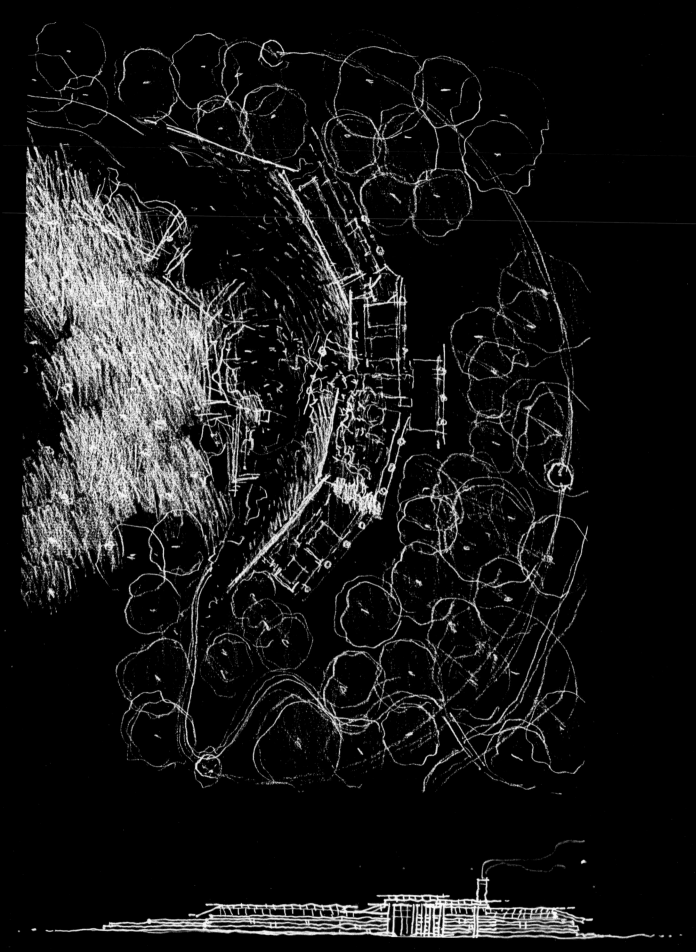

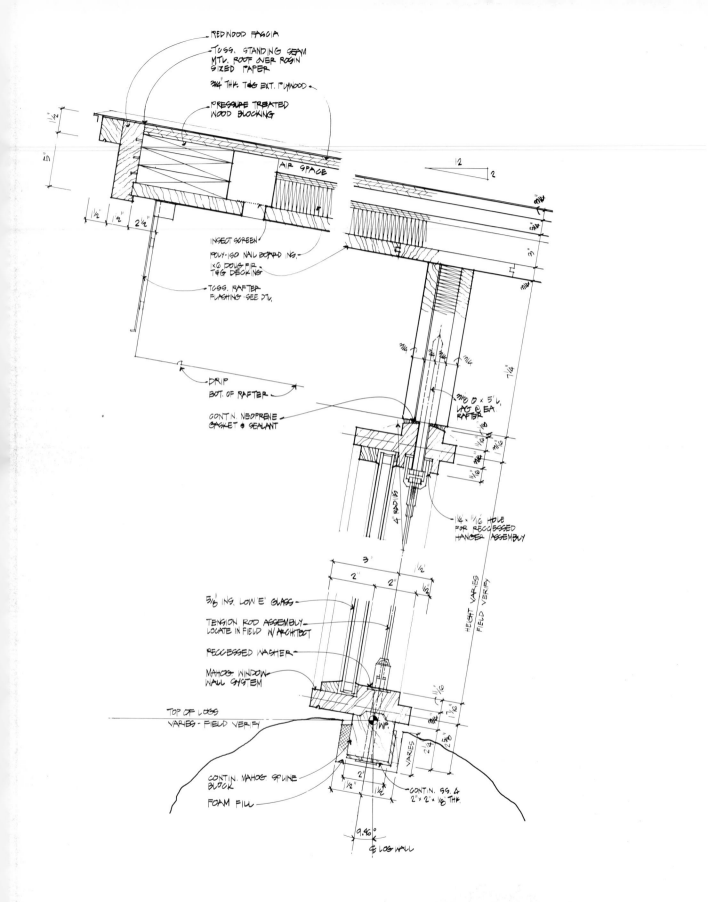

REDWOOD FASCIA

T.O.S.G. STANDING SEAM
MTL. ROOF OVER ROSIN
SIZED PAPER

3/4" THK. T&G EXT. PLYWOOD

PRESSURE TREATED
WOOD BLOCKING

AIR SPACE

12
2

INSECT SCREEN

POLY-ISO NAIL BOARD INS.

1X6 DOUG FIR
T&G DECKING

T.O.S.G. RAFTER
FLASHING · SEE DTL.

DRIP

BOT. OF RAFTER

CONT'N. NEOPRENE
GASKET & SEALANT

3/4" Ø X 5" L,
LAG @ EA
RAFTER

1/4" X 1/16" HOLE
FOR RECCESSED
HANGER ASSEMBLY

4" RADIUS

HEIGHT VARIES
FIELD VERIFY

3"
2"   1/2"

5/8" ING. LOW 'E' GLASS

TENSION ROD ASSEMBLY
LOCATE IN FIELD W/ARCHITECT

RECCESSED WASHER

MAHOG. WINDOW
WALL SYSTEM

TOP OF LOGS
VARIES · FIELD VERIFY

WP

VARIES   2 1/4"   2 1/2"

CONT'N. MAHOG SPLINE
BLOCK

FOAM FILL

2"
1/2"   1/2"

CONT'N. SS. &
2" X 2" X 1/8" THK.

9.46°

₵ LOG WALL

Section at north log wall clerestory window (above) Construction process (previous spread and following page)

22 23 24 25 26 Aerial view (previous spread) Approach
from the north (left) Log wall extending northwest from pool,
showing lead shrouds (top) Detail: log and stone wall (second
from top) North wall, pool pavilion (second from bottom)
Sketch: log wall (bottom)

27 28 29 Forecourt (previous spread) Log wall and roof at forecourt (opposite page) Detail: clerestory window and roof overhang outside pool (above)

30 31 32 Log wall and roof at forecourt (previous spread) Entry (left and right) Construction details: log wall elevations (below)

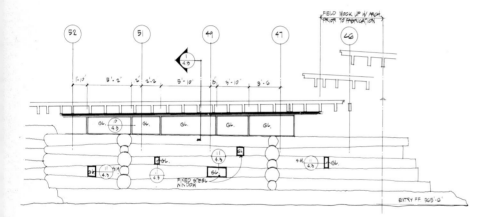

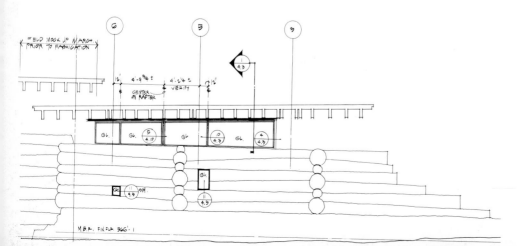

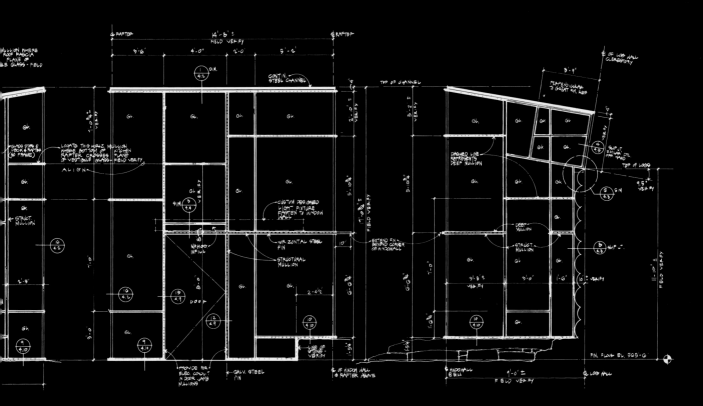

33 View from entry along north wall (left)   Construction details: entry vestibule windows (above)

37 38 39 Window wall in living space (top left)
Detail at glass-to-stone joint (middle left)
Column-beam connection in living space (right)
Sketches: column bases at wood and stone floors
(bottom left)

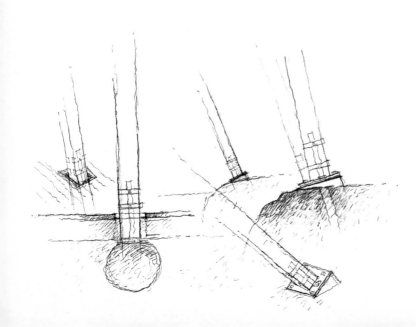

40 41 42 43 Living space (previous spread) Fireplace tools (upper left) Detail: quartzite stone (lower left) Living space ceiling at skylight (right)

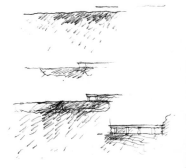

44 45 46 View west to master bedroom from hall (left) View to master bedroom hall from living space (above, top) Detail: transition from stone ledge to wood floor (above, bottom) Sketches: wood floor "floats" over stone ledge (above, middle)

47 48 49 South wall, master bedroom (upper left) Detail: master bedroom shelving (lower left) View east to study from master bedroom (right)

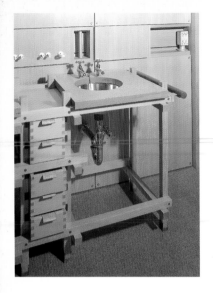

50 51 52 53 View west to master bedroom from hall to study (previous spread left) Detail: master bedroom (previous spread right) Details: bathroom vanity (photographs and drawings)

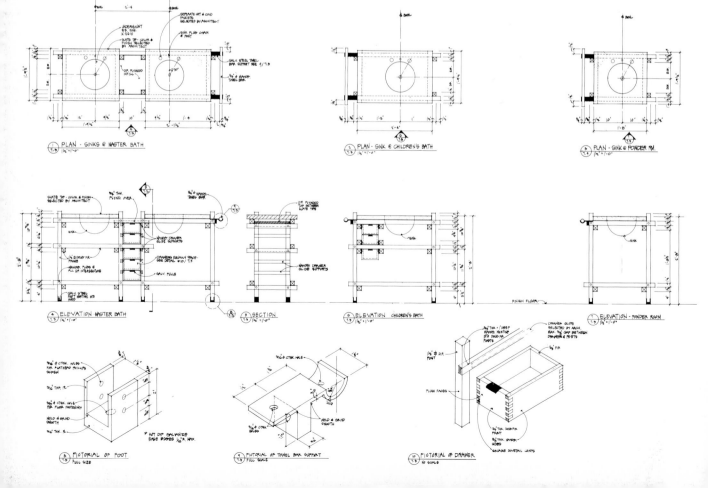

54 55 56 Study with Asplund chair and original sketch (left and upper right) Study, west wall (lower right)

57 58 59 60 61 Windows in log wall with clerestory window above (top) View from master bedroom hall toward entry (middle) Detail: log ends, hall to master bedroom (bottom) Detail: window in log wall (opposite page) Clerestory windows and column-beam connections in living space (following spread)

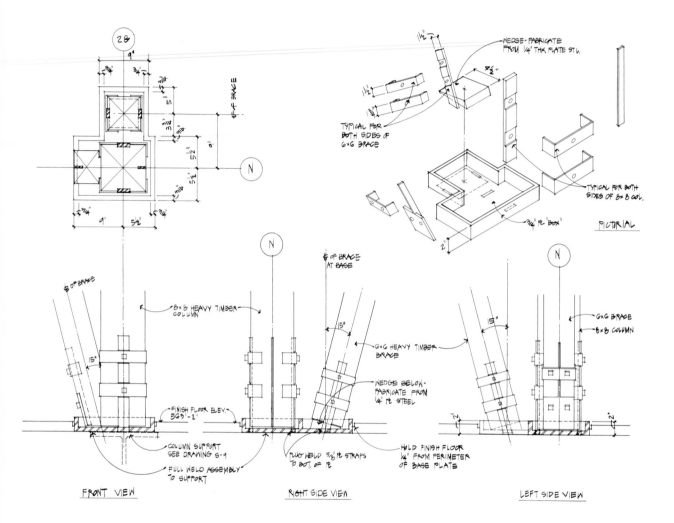

2θ

9"

£ OF BRACE

N

WEDGE-FABRICATE FROM ¼" THK. PLATE STL.

TYPICAL FOR BOTH SIDES OF 6×6 BRACE

4½"

½"

½"

¾"

TYPICAL FOR BOTH SIDES OF 8×8 COL.

¾" PL 'BOX'

2"

PICTORIAL

£ OF BRACE

8×8 HEAVY TIMBER COLUMN

15°

FINISH FLOOR ELEV. 563'-2"

COLUMN SUPPORT SEE DRAWING S-9

FULL WELD ASSEMBLY TO SUPPORT

FRONT VIEW

N

£ OF BRACE AT BASE

15°

6×6 HEAVY TIMBER BRACE

WEDGE BELOW - FABRICATE FROM ¼" PL STEEL

PLUG WELD ⅜" PL STRAPS TO BOT. OF PL

HOLD FINISH FLOOR ¼" FROM PERIMETER OF BASE PLATE

RIGHT SIDE VIEW

N

15°

6×6 BRACE

8×8 COLUMN

2"

2"

LEFT SIDE VIEW

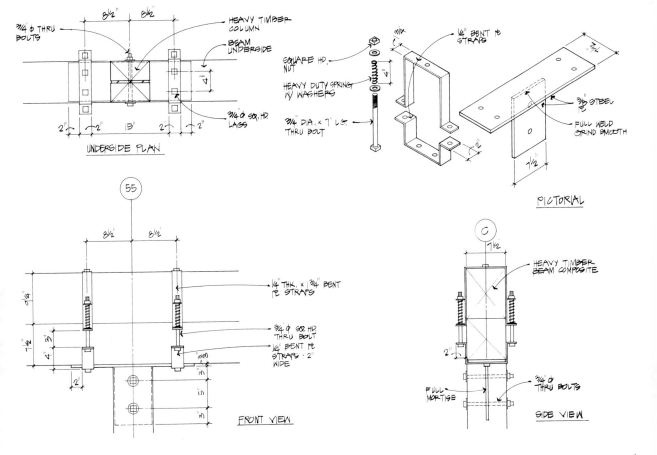

³⁄₄ Ø THRU BOLTS

8½" 8½"

HEAVY TIMBER COLUMN

BEAM UNDERSIDE

SQUARE HD. NUT

HEAVY DUTY SPRING W/ WASHERS

¼" BENT ₽ STRAPS

³⁄₈" STEEL

FULL WELD GRIND SMOOTH

³⁄₄ DIA. × 7" LG. THRU BOLT

2" 2" 13" 2" 2"

³⁄₄ Ø SQ. HD. LAGS

4"

7½"

UNDERSIDE PLAN

PICTORIAL

55

8½" 8½"

9¼"

7½"

3"

4"

2"

¼" THK. × 3⁄4 BENT ₽ STRAPS

³⁄₄ Ø SQ. HD. THRU BOLT

¼" BENT ₽ STRAPS · 2" WIDE

3"

5"

3"

FRONT VIEW

C

7½"

HEAVY TIMBER BEAM COMPOSITE

2"

FULL MORTISE

³⁄₄ Ø THRU BOLTS

SIDE VIEW

62 Column base at stone ledge in living space (previous foldout) Column-beam connections (above) Column bases at wood floors (opposite page)

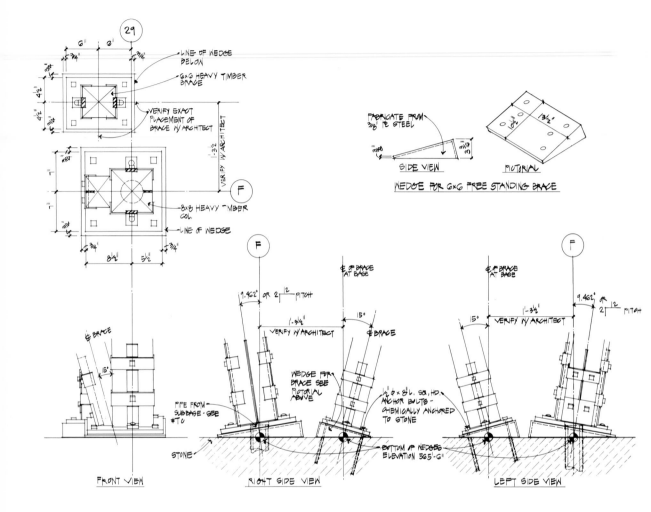

Column bases at stone floors and ledge (opposite page) Column bases at stone floors and ledge (above)

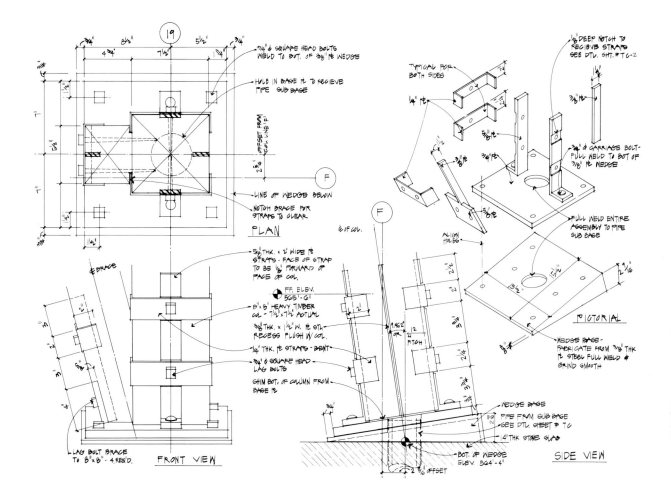

PLAN

⌀19

3/4" ∅ SQUARE HEAD BOLTS WELD TO BOT. OF 3/8" ℞ WEDGE

HOLE IN BASE ℞ TO RECIEVE PIPE SUB BASE

OFFSET FROM COL. LINE "F"

F

LINE OF WEDGE BELOW

NOTCH BRACE FOR STRAPS TO CLEAR

TYPICAL FOR BOTH SIDES

1/4" ℞

5/8" ℞

3/8" ℞

3/4" ℞

1/8" DEEP NOTCH TO RECIEVE STRAPS SEE DTL. SHT. # TC-2

3/8" ℞

3/4" ∅ CARRIAGE BOLT- FULL WELD TO BOT OF 3/8" ℞ WEDGE

FULL WELD ENTIRE ASSEMBLY TO PIPE SUB BASE

ALIGN HOLES

PICTORIAL

WEDGE BASE - FABRICATE FROM 3/8" THK ℞ STEEL FULL WELD & GRIND SMOOTH

5/8" THK. x 2" WIDE ℞ STRAPS - FACE OF STRAP TO BE 1/8" FORWARD OF FACE OF COL.

FF. ELEV. 565'-6"

8" x 8" HEAVY TIMBER COL - 7 1/2" x 7 1/2" ACTUAL

3/8" THK. x 1 1/2" W. ℞ STL. RECESS FLUSH W/ COL.

1/4" THK. ℞ STRAPS - BENT

3/4" ∅ SQUARE HEAD LAG BOLTS

SHIM BOT. OF COLUMN FROM BASE ℞

F

9.462" OR 2 1/2" PITCH

WEDGE BASE

PIPE FROM SUB BASE SEE DTL. SHEET # TC

4" THK. STONE SLAB

BOT. OF WEDGE ELEV. 564'-4"

2 3/16 OFFSET

SIDE VIEW

LAG BOLT BRACE TO 8" x 8" - 4 REQ'D.

FRONT VIEW

63 64 65 66 67 68 69 70 71 Column bases at wood floor in living space (previous foldout) Living space and kitchen from master bedroom hall (previous spread) Details: desk in living space (left and below) Detail: low table in living space (right)

72 73 74 View from living space toward kitchen and entry (left) Detail at window wall in living space (upper right) Detail: window wall stiffener (lower right)

75 76 77 Detail at kitchen (above) Kitchen (right) Screened porch (following spread)

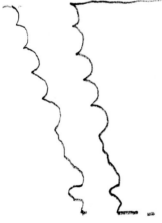

80 81 82 "Mouse bite" door from pool, photographs and sketch (above) Hall at children's bedrooms; pool through "mouse bite" door (right)

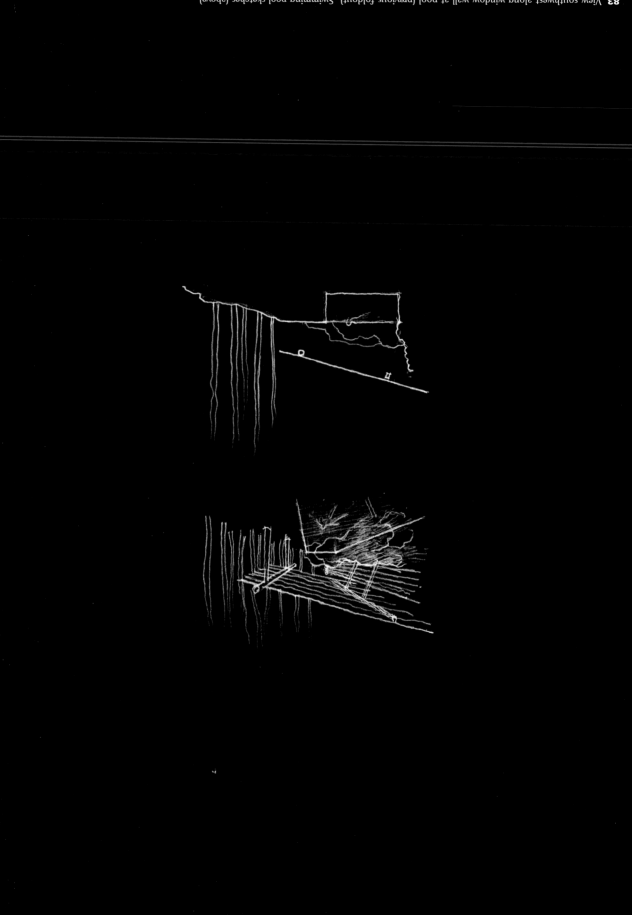

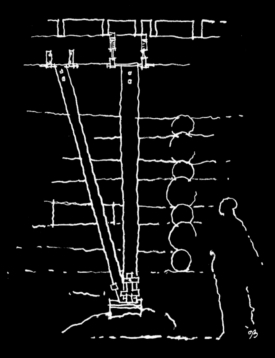

84 85 Swimming pool (left) Sketch: columns and beams with log wall (above) View along window wall at pool (following foldout)

90 91 92 View north to house from stream (upper left) View east along south face of house (lower left) South wall at living space (right)

CONTIN. STAINLESS STL.
CHANNEL - PAINTED.
SCREW FASTEN TO EACH RAF

COMPOSITE
BEAM
GLAZE TO BM. UNDERSIDE

LINE OF
STONE WALL

SCRIBE HORIZ.
MULLIONS TIGHT
TO STONE

DASHED LINE
REPRESENTS
DEEP MULLION

FINISH FLOOR
EL. 563'-2"

GL. GL. GL.

GL. GL.

GL.

GL. GL.

GL. GL.

10 ELEVATION
4.1 GREAT RM

11 ELEVATIO
4.1 GREAT RM

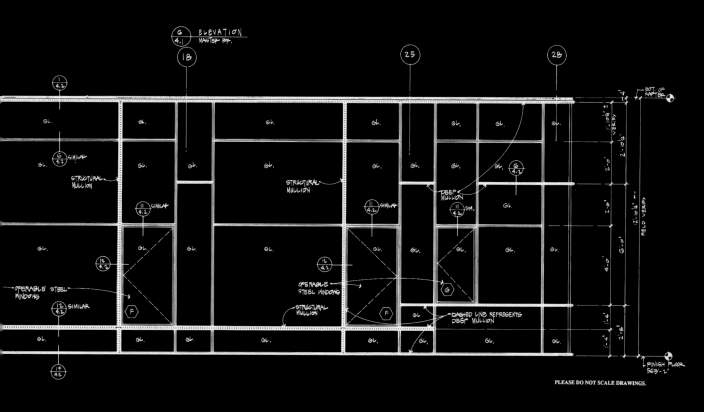

93 94 95 Detail: south wall at living space (left) West end (following spread left) West end at dusk (following spread right) Window details (above)

96 97 98 99 100 Detail: lead shrouds on log wall (left) Above: Wall detail (top) Kitchen window from porch (second from top) Detail: master bedroom, west wall (second from bottom) Detail: southwest corner of master bedroom (bottom)

Project Name: Ledge House
Owner: Withheld at owner's request
Location: The mountains of rural Maryland
Architect: Bohlin Cywinski Jackson
                Architecture Planning Interior Design
                Wilkes-Barre / Pittsburgh / Philadelphia /
                Seattle

8 West Market Street
Suite 1200, Wilkes-Barre, PA 18701
570-825-8756

307 Fourth Avenue
Pittsburgh, PA 15222
412-765-3890

123 South Broad Street
Philadelphia, PA 19109
215-790-5900

1932 First Avenue
Suite 916, Seattle, WA 98101
206-256-0862

Honor Award, American Institute of Architects, 1996
Merit Award, American Wood Council, 1996
Silver Award for Design Excellence, Pennsylvania Society
of Architects, 1995

Design Team:	Peter Q. Bohlin, FAIA, principal in charge	Building Area:	4,250 square feet
	Joseph N. Biondo, AIA, project manager	Date of Design:	1992-1996
	Alan Purvis, project team	Date of Completion:	Spring 1996

Consultants:	Structural Engineer:	E. D. Pons & Associates, Inc.
	Mechanical Engineer:	Martin / Rogers / Associates
	Electrical Engineer:	Martin / Rogers / Associates
	Landscape Architect:	Allan D. Garnaas Associates

General Contractor:	Currey's Custom Homes
	10324-B Harmony Road
	Myersville, MD 21773
	301-293-0991

Cedar Log Installer:	Town & Country Cedar Homes
	4772 U.S. 131 South
	Petosky, MI 49770
	616-347-4360

Bohlin Cywinski Jackson, founded in 1965, currently has offices in Wilkes-Barre, Pittsburgh, Philadelphia and Seattle. The firm's w

is known for its commitment to particularity of place and user and an extraordinary aesthetic based on a quiet rigor which is b

intellectual and intuitive. ▍ The firm's five principals, twenty-two associates and total staff of ninety practice architecture and d

a range of related services. Its breadth and depth of skills and experience enable the practice to address a wide range of challeng

difficult sites, demanding budgets and time constraints, unusual technological requirements, and the integration of new construc

with existing buildings and contexts. The firm aims to respond to the particular circumstances in each situation, alive to the subtle

of place—man-made or natural—to the varied natures of client and user, to the character of institutions, and to the mean

construction. ▍ While Bohlin Cywinski Jackson has become noted for a broad range of work, including large assignments for univers

and corporations such as Carnegie Mellon University's Software Engineering Institute and Pixar Animation Studios, the firm continue

design noteworthy houses that vary greatly in scale and circumstance. These houses have often pointed the way toward

architecture of the firm's larger commissions. ▍ Bohlin Cywinski Jackson has received more than 170 regional, national and internati

awards for design, and in 1994 received the national Architecture Firm Award from the American Institute of Architects. The firm's

is published in professional journals worldwide.

From left: Alan Purvis, Peter Bohlin, Joseph Biondo

Originally from Buenos Aires, Oscar Riera Ojeda is an editor and designer who practices in the United States, South America and Europe from his office in Boston. He is vice-director of the Spanish-Argentinian magazine *Casas Internacional,* and is the creator of several series of architectural publications for Rockport Publishers in addition to the *Single Building* series, including *Ten Houses, Contemporary World Architects, Architecture in Detail* and *Art and Architecture.* Other architectural publications include the *New American* series for the Whitney Library of Design, as well as several monographs on the work of renowned architects.

The text was edited by Mark Denton, an architect practicing in Santa Monica, California and New London, Connecticut.

photographic credits

◄ Reference plans
showing photograph
vantage points
inside

Additional plans
inside back cover ►►